Filibusters

By Anita Croy

Published in 2019 by
Lucent Press, an Imprint of Greenhaven Publishing, LLC
353 3rd Avenue
Suite 255
New York, NY 10010

For Brown Bear Books Ltd
Editorial Director: Lindsey Lowe
Managing Editor: Tim Cooke
Designer: Lynne Lennon
Design Manager: Keith Davis
Picture Manager: Sophie Mortimer
Children's Publisher: Anne O'Daly

Picture Credits
Front cover: Robert Daemmrich Photography Inc/Corbis Historical/Getty Images
Interior: Alamy: Bob Daemmrich, 34, SuperStock/Richard Cummins, 17; **Getty Images:** Chip Somodevilla,
45; **iStock:** 221A, 16, Ginos Photos, 37, Luna Marina, 11, nkbimages, 42, subjug, 18; **Library of Congress:** 8,
9; **Public Domain:** 7, Al Cook, 6, Lyndon Baines Johnson Library, 28, National Board of Review Magazine/
Columbia Pictures, 35, Scrumshus, 41, collection of Supreme Court/Franz Jantzen, 29, US Government/
Senate, 5, 30, US Senage 11th Congress, Senate Photo Studio, 4, WHPO/Cecil Stoughton, 20; **Shutterstock:**
Andy Dean Photography, 39, Arindam Banerjee, 40, Ruth Black, 13, BlueSkyImage, 38, Orhan Cam, 19,
Andrew Cline, 43, Julie Clopper, 24, Diego G Diaz, 27, Everett Historical, 10, 12, Flexey, 25, Hurst Photo, 15,
Gina Jacobs, 36, Just2shutter, 21, Stephen Moehle, 32, Gino Santa-Maria, 23, Ron Foster Sharif, 22, Jeffrey J
Snyder, 26, Joseph Sohm, 14, J Stone, 31, Albert H Telch, 33, Katherine Welles, 44.

Brown Bear Books has made every attempt to contact the copyright holders.
If you have any information please contact licensing@brownbearbooks.co.uk

Cataloging-in-Publication Data

Names: Croy, Anita.
Title: Filibusters / Anita Croy.
Description: New York : Lucent Press, 2019. | Series: Inside American politics | Includes glossary and index.
Identifiers: ISBN 9781534566682 (pbk.) | ISBN 9781534566699 (library bound) |
ISBN 9781534566705 (ebook)
Subjects: LCSH: Filibusters (Political science)–United States–Juvenile literature. |
Communication in politics–Juvenile literature. | United States. Congress. Senate–Juvenile literature. |
United States. Congress–Juvenile literature.
Classification: LCC JF519.C79 2019 | DDC 320.473′04–dc23

Printed in the United States of America

CPSIA compliance information:Batch #BW19KL: For further information contact Greenhaven Publishing LLC, New York, New York at 1-844-317-7404.

Please visit our website, www.greenhavenpublishing.com. For a free color catalog of all our
high-quality books, call toll free 1-844-317-7404 or fax 1-844-317-7405.

Contents

TALK UNTIL
YOU DROP!

The US Senate is the senior chamber of Congress. It is a place for serious debate. Senators vote on hundreds of new laws every year. So imagine walking into the Senate chamber to find a senator reading out recipes for oyster dishes, or entries from the Washington, D.C., phone book. Or how about a senator reading a bedtime story to his daughters, who are watching on TV at home? Remarkably, these methods have all been used to delay **debate** in the Senate. This delaying tactic is called a filibuster. It usually means that a senator or group of senators is trying to prevent a law from being passed.

Every state has two senators in the US Senate, whatever its size.
The arrangement is meant to protect the voices of smaller states.

The filibuster has been part of Senate proceedings since 1805. It originally guaranteed senators the right to speak for as long as they wanted about any issue. A filibuster could only be stopped if the speaker left the floor, or if a so-called super majority of two-thirds of senators voted to end the debate.

A Changing Tactic

The way the filibuster is used has changed. In the past, senators had to stand up in the chamber and speak without stopping. It was physically and mentally demanding, so filibusters were relatively rare. Today, a filibuster can be prevented from making it to the Senate floor. If one party in the Senate informs the other party that it has the support of enough senators to block a piece of **legislation** by stopping a super majority from forcing it through, that legislation is halted without anyone having to stand up and filibuster in the chamber. This is known as a virtual filibuster.

The filibuster was introduced to Congress early in the 1800s. For about 200 years, it was a rarely used political tactic.

George Orwell's novel 1984 is about a future state where everyone is under constant surveillance.

Other countries also use the filibuster. In March 2016, South Korean senators set a world record of 192 hours of filibustering to delay a bill they believed would give too many powers to the **intelligence services**. The filibuster lasted more than nine days. The senators wore sneakers because they were on their feet for so long. To underline their objection to state control, some senators read passages from the book *1984*, by the British writer George Orwell. Even after all their efforts, the filibuster failed. The senators would have needed to keep on speaking for another eight days to use up all the time allocated for discussing the bill.

WHAT DO YOU THINK?

A filibuster is a test of physical stamina. Some senators, however, are old and may not be physically strong. In what other ways might they be empowered to make a protest on the floor of the Senate?

The Power of the People

In ancient Rome in the first century BC, the politician and statesman Cato the Younger was known for public speaking. He would often speak in the Senate, or government council, until it closed at sunset to prevent senators from voting on an issue. In 60 BC, Cato spoke until sunset in an effort to stop Julius Caesar, his sworn enemy, from seizing power in Rome. Although the Senate did not give Caesar power, he seized control of Rome anyway.

The Roman Senate began its meetings at dawn and had to end by nightfall. All senators had the right to speak, so it was possible to talk so long that time ran out before a vote could be held.

Chapter 2

WHAT IS A FILIBUSTER?

The US Constitution does not include any mention of filibustering. The practice of letting senators voice their displeasure about a bill by talking on the Senate floor is thought to have been adopted almost by accident, thanks to the third vice president, Aaron Burr. Today, Burr is best remembered as the man who killed Alexander Hamilton, one of the Founding Fathers, in a duel in 1804. But as vice president, Burr presided over the Senate.

In 1805, Burr suggested that the Senate should get rid of a rule known as the previous question rule. This rule was a way to stop any Senate debate and force a vote. Burr argued that it was

Aaron Burr rejected the use of the previous question rule, by which a simple majority could force a vote in the House or Senate.

not really needed. In 1806, the Senate followed Burr's advice and dropped the previous question rule. It was unclear how the Senate could now force a debate to a vote.

Thirty years later, in 1841, a bill proposed by Senator Henry Clay was blocked by the Democratic minority. Clay threatened to change Senate rules to allow his Whig Party to vote to end the debate. Democrats continued the debate, delaying the bill by 10 days. The Senate's right to unlimited debate was confirmed—which made it possible for a long enough filibuster to prevent a vote from taking place.

Henry Clay was renowned for his ability to make deals and use procedures to get legislation passed into laws.

Voting in the House

To begin with, the House of Representatives also had unlimited debates. As the United States expanded west, however, representatives of new states joined the House. Now, there was not enough time for everyone to speak in the House. In 1842, a new rule limited the length of House debates, which could be ended by a simple majority vote.

The word "filibuster" was first used in the 1850s. It comes from a Dutch word *vrijbuiter*, or freebooter, a kind of pirate. Filibustering entered the Senate rule book in 1856, which officially allowed for unlimited debate on the Senate floor in certain circumstances.

A freebooter was a type of pirate who launched illegal attacks on ships from other nations.

Rule 22

The rules remained unchanged until 1917. During World War I (1914–1918), President Woodrow Wilson was prevented from adopting war measures such as arming US merchant ships. A few antiwar members of the Senate used a filibuster to delay a vote on Wilson's proposals. Wilson complained that "A little group of willful men representing no opinion but their own, have rendered the great government of the United States helpless and contemptible." He urged the Senate to close a debate if a two-thirds majority voted to end it. The Senate adopted this measure as Rule 22, otherwise known as "cloture." It was used for the first time in 1919, when the Senate ended a filibuster against the Treaty of Versailles.

Over the next five decades, the Senate tried but failed to use cloture. It was difficult to secure a two-thirds majority, so filibusters remained an effective way to block legislation. During the 1950s and 1960s, Southern senators used filibusters to block civil rights legislation, including anti-**lynching** legislation. The longest filibuster was made by South Carolina Senator J. Strom Thurmond against the 1957 Civil Rights Act. It lasted 24 hours 18 minutes.

More Changes

In 1975, the Senate voted to reduce the number of votes required for cloture from two-thirds (67) to three-fifths (60) of the senators. Another change allowed the Senate to conduct other business while a filibuster was underway. That stopped a filibuster from blocking the whole legislative process.

The US Senate rejected the two-thirds law, which made it difficult to stop a filibuster.

WHAT DO YOU THINK?

Strom Thurmond staged the longest-ever filibuster to delay legislation that gave equal civil rights to all Americans. Does knowing his purpose make you look at his filibuster in a different way? If so, how?

President Woodrow Wilson throws the first pitch at a baseball game. Although Wilson introduced Rule 22 to try to prevent filibusters, they became more frequent events in the Senate.

The Virtual Filibuster

Today, senators rarely stand up in the Senate to filibuster. They use a virtual filibuster simply by announcing their intention to filibuster. If 60 senators do not cloture the filibuster, the legislation is shelved.

Since Rule 22 was introduced in 1917, the filibuster has been used 1,300 times. The majority of filibusters have taken place since 1975, mostly in the 2000s. Nearly 600 filibusters were used between 2006 and 2018.

WHAT DO YOU THINK?

A virtual filibuster can prevent legislation being debated in the Senate. How could you justify this as an acceptable part of a democratic system?

THE POWER OF THE PEOPLE

There are rules to filibustering. A senator can talk about anything, but if he or she sits down, or leaves the Senate floor, the filibuster is over. During the filibuster, the senator may only eat hard candy from the "candy desk" in the chamber and drink only water or milk. They are not allowed to pause, but they can take a break by getting another senator to ask them questions. They definitely cannot take a bathroom break.

Since the 1960s, it has been traditional for a senator to keep his or her desk drawer filled with candy for his colleagues. The "candy desk" is not just for filibusters, but for any senator with a sweet tooth.

Chapter 3

FILIBUSTERS
IN HISTORY

Filibustering or threatening to filibuster is relatively common today, but for a long time it was used relatively sparingly. When it was used, therefore, a filibuster often made the headlines. In fact, senators who filibustered were often seeking greater publicity for an issue rather than actually hoping to change legislation. The press was quick to report the different kinds that tactics senators used in order to stay on their feet and keep talking and talking.

A Deadly Drink

One of the most famous filibusters happened before the introduction of cloture in 1917. It ended in suspicion that someone had tried to stop Wisconsin Senator Bob La Follette in a far more dramatic way than through cloture.

Republican Senator Rand Paul has filibustered twice in the Senate since 2013, putting him in a long line of filibustering politicians from both parties.

In 1908, La Follette used a filibuster to try to prevent the Senate from adopting a report that he believed favored the concerns of big business over those of the workers. It was the last session of the Senate before it broke for the summer vacation, and most senators were eager to end the debate.

By the early hours of May 30, 1908, La Follette had been speaking for 12 hours. He showed no signs of stopping, but he needed some refreshment. He asked for a turkey sandwich and a glass of eggnog to keep him going. What happened next is a matter of record, although the precise circumstances remain mysterious.

Eggnog is a mixture of raw eggs and milk. Water and milk are the only drinks that can be consumed during a filibuster.

Shortly before 1:00 a.m., La Follette took a sip of his eggnog, but something about it did not taste right. He left the rest of the glass and kept on talking, but soon started to feel ill and broke out in sweat. By 7:00 a.m. he was so ill he could not carry on. He was replaced by a colleague after filibustering for 18 hours and 23 minutes—a record for an individual speaker that would last for more than 50 years.

When the contents of the glass were later analyzed, they were shown to be full of toxic **bacteria**. There was a chance that the eggnog would have killed La Follette if he had consumed it all. Although some conspiracy theories suggested he was deliberately poisoned, the likelihood is that the unrefrigerated milk and eggs had gone rotten in the heat of the Washington, D.C., summer.

It's All Shakespeare to Me!

During the Great Depression of the 1930s, one of the Senate's most colorful members was Huey Long, from Louisiana. Long was a passionate speaker who was known for his criticism of the policies of his fellow Democrat, President Franklin D. Roosevelt. On August 21, 1935, Long filibustered for 15 hours and 30 minutes. He was trying to prevent his opponents within the Democratic Party from getting **lucrative** jobs with the National Recovery Administration (NRA). The NRA was a federal agency that had been set up by Roosevelt to encourage economic growth and create jobs.

During his filibuster, Huey Long filled time by reading out passages from the plays of William Shakespeare.

First, Long analyzed the Constitution. Then, he read from the plays of William Shakespeare. Next, he read out recipes for fried oysters and salad dressing. Long's filibuster only ended when he had to use the bathroom. It was his last major speech. Long was **assassinated** by the relative of a rival politician the next month.

Blocking Civil Rights

J. Strom Thurmond set the record for the longest filibuster in Senate history in 1957. He spoke for 24 hours and 18 minutes against the Civil Rights Act. Thurmond was a conservative Democrat from South Carolina, where civil rights legislation was viewed with suspicion.

A statue of Strom Thurmond stands on the grounds of the State Capitol in Columbia, South Carolina.

WHAT DO YOU THINK?

Some people say that politicians only use filibustering to call attention to themselves. How could the filibuster rules be changed to prevent this from happening?

Strom Thurmond easily broke the previous record for continuous speaking, which had been set by the Oregon Senator Wayne Morse in 1953. Morse had spoken for 22 hours and 26 minutes against "tideland" legislation. The act, which eventually passed, gave states the right to extract oil and other resources found in the states' coastal waters.

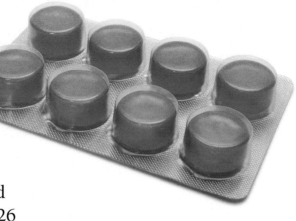

Thurmond used throat lozenges to try to protect himself against losing his voice.

Senators using the filibuster are not allowed to leave the floor for any reason. Thurmond prepared carefully for his marathon filibuster. Before he went to the Senate for the debate, he took a steam bath. This sweated out much of the fluid in his body, just in case he might need the bathroom. He also brought a steak sandwich, throat lozenges, and malted milk tablets into the Senate chamber.

━ WHAT DO YOU THINK? ━

Imagine you were going to try to filibuster for many hours, like Strom Thurmond. What preparations would you make? What would you bring to the chamber to help you make it through the experience?

THE POWER OF THE PEOPLE

Filibusters are not only used to slow the passing of bills. Senators have increasingly used the tactic to block the president's nominees for federal positions that require Senate confirmation. The tactic is particularly used to block nominations for Supreme Court justices. In 1968, a coalition of Southern Democrats and Republicans filibustered President Lyndon B. Johnson's nomination for Chief Justice, Abe Fortas. They feared Fortas was not truly independent. This was the first time a filibuster had stopped a president's nomination. It set a precedent that continues today.

The nine justices of the US Supreme Court hold their positions for life, so the president's nomination of a new justice has a long-lasting influence.

During Thurmond's long filibuster, senators slept on cots borrowed from a hotel. Thurmond spoke about anything he could think of. At one stage, he read out his grandmother's recipe for biscuits. Despite his performance, however, he failed to stop the act. A few years later, Southern senators also held up the 1964 Civil Rights Act. It was delayed from February to June by filibusters, before finally becoming law.

The Singing Senator

In 1986, New York Senator Alfonse D'Amato made the second-longest solo filibuster when he spoke for 23 hours and 30 minutes against a military bill. D'Amato resorted to reading aloud from the District of Columbia phone book.

President Lyndon B. Johnson signs the Civil Rights Act in 1964, after a series of filibusters by Southern senators who resisted allowing African Americans being granted equal rights.

Alfonse D'Amato tried unsuccessfully to keep the Smith Corona typewriter company from moving its operations from New York to Mexico by offering tax concessions.

Six years later, D'Amato filibustered again. On October 5, 1992, he filibustered for 15 hours and 14 minutes in an attempt to save more than 800 jobs in a New York typewriter company. The company had announced that it was going to relocate to Mexico in order to reduce costs. As part of his filibuster, the senator sang the 1939 popular song "South of the Border (Down Mexico Way)." This was the first filibuster broadcast live on television, and D'Amato kept his TV audience in mind. He timed his filibuster so it did not interrupt any other Senate business and began speaking at dinnertime so that he could continue through the night. He only stopped the next day, when the Senate ended its session for the year.

━ WHAT DO YOU THINK? ━

Alfonse D'Amato filibustered to try to save jobs for his electors. Does it make a difference whether a filibuster is carried out for ideological reasons or simply for practical or selfish purposes? In what way?

Chapter 4

FILIBUSTERS TODAY

A filibuster or the threat of a filibuster sets off a complex chain of events. It can bring Senate procedures to a halt for up to a week, preventing senators from working on other pressing business. This has become more important in the last decade, because the number of filibusters has increased dramatically.

When Barack Obama became president, he had the support of a Democratic Congress. In the later part of his presidency, however, he was often blocked by a Republican Congress.

A Common Event

Barack Obama began the first of his two terms as president in 2009. Since then, the Senate has seen around 600 filibusters. As his opponents used filibusters to block his laws, Obama argued that the process was being used to prevent ideas from being heard.

Democrat Bernie Sanders used a long speech to try to force President Obama to impose higher taxes on the wealthiest Americans.

In 2013, Obama said, "Filibustering … not a responsible way to govern … It is rather used as a reckless and relentless tool to grind all business to a halt." Obama complained that this was very different from the filibuster's original purpose of promoting discussion among senators. One estimate is that, at various times during Obama's administration, filibusters allowed senators representing as few as 11 percent of Americans to prevent the Senate from doing any business.

Not a Filibuster …

One attempt to delay President Obama's program came in December 2010 from his own Democratic Party. Senator Bernie Sanders of Vermont, who would run in the 2015 primaries to become the Democratic presidential candidate, spoke to protest that the president was going to water down his proposed tax cuts to gain Republican support.

Speaking for more than eight hours, Senator Sanders read out letters from his constituents. They had been hit hard by the 2008 global **recession**, and their letters described their hardship. Sanders was not actually stopping any bill, however, so although his speech was remarkably long, it was not technically a filibuster.

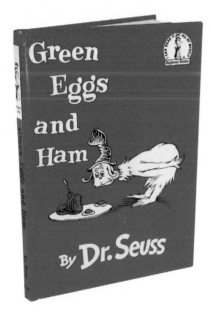

After he read Dr. Seuss, Ted Cruz told his daughters via TV, "Brush your teeth, say your prayers, and Daddy's going to be home soon."

Green Eggs and Ham

Obama faced a conventional filibuster in 2013, when Republican senator Ted Cruz of Texas took to the Senate floor. Cruz wanted to halt the president's health care reforms. His marathon speech lasted more than 21 hours, going past his children's bedtime. Not wanting to miss the chance to read his kids their bedtime story, Cruz read out Dr. Seuss's *Green Eggs and Ham*. Thanks to the live Senate broadcast, his daughters heard their dad reading them a story.

WHAT DO YOU THINK?

Ted Cruz got to broadcast to his children thanks to continuous TV coverage of the Senate. In what ways is it beneficial that Americans are able to watch their politicians in action?

Droning On

Another filibuster in 2013 came from the Kentucky Senator Rand Paul. Paul's speech was technically about the potential use of unmanned aerial **drones** on US soil. While the senator was interested in drones and their future potential, however, the real reason for Senator Paul's filibuster was because he wanted to delay the Senate confirmation of Obama's new Director of the Central Intelligence Agency (CIA), John O'Brennan.

Drones were the apparent subject of Rand Paul's filibuster—but its real target was very different.

Paul's filibuster lasted for 13 hours. He told senators that he wanted to carry on for another 12 hours to break Strom Thurmond's record. However, he joked, "I've discovered that there are some limits to filibustering and I am going to have to take care of one of those in a few minutes." With that, he headed for the bathroom.

Gun Control

In the last year of his administration, President Obama faced a filibuster about guns. Although he supported gun control, during the president's eight years in office, the number of mass shootings across the United States had risen.

Students in Tucson, Arizona, demonstrate in favor of increased gun control after a mass shooting in Florida in 2018.

In June 2016, a mass shooting in Orlando, Florida, left 49 people dead and 53 wounded. In response, Senator Chris Murphy from Connecticut, a veteran campaigner against gun violence, filibustered in the US Senate for almost 15 hours to try to force Congress to debate gun control. Murphy ended his filibuster after Senate leaders agreed to hold votes on two measures for improving gun safety: preventing suspected terrorists from getting hold of guns and extending background checks on gun purchasers.

Going nuclear

During the Obama administration, the Senate majority developed a new, and highly controversial, tactic to use against a filibuster. This was the so-called nuclear option.

WHAT DO YOU THINK?

Many people believe gun rights organizations have too much power over US politicians. In what way could you encourage politicians to debate gun laws more seriously?

THE POWER OF THE PEOPLE

In February 2018, Minority Leader of the House Nancy Pelosi made a speech that lasted more than eight hours. She delayed a budget deal in order to try to force Republicans to debate immigration, particularly the future of young immigrants brought to the United States illegally by their parents. Pelosi read out letters from these so-called **Dreamers**. She wanted to publicize the contribution many had made to the United States. Reading their testimonies gave a voice to people whose experiences had long been marginalized.

Protestors against the end of Deferred Action for Childhood Arrivals (DACA), which allowed the Dreamers to remain in the United States, gather in Portland, Oregon, in September 2017.

27

Former vice president Richard M. Nixon (left) meets with President Lyndon B. Johnson in 1969.

The nuclear option allows the Senate to override the 60-vote rule and vote by a simple majority on any business being delayed by a minority. The idea was first suggested in 1957 by Vice President Richard M. Nixon, but the procedure was not used until 2013, by Democrat Harry Reid, who was the Senate Majority Leader. Reid claimed Republicans were obstructing Senate business as judges in federal courts and by refusing to confirm Obama's nominees for federal posts.

━ WHAT DO YOU THINK? ━

The nuclear option makes it easier for a president to appoint potentially controversial officials and judges. Why might a president appoint a divisive figure rather than someone who attracts broad, **bipartisan** support?

The nuclear option made it easier for presidents to get their nominees through the Senate. In the past, presidents tended to select appointees acceptable to both parties in order to secure confirmation. Now, however, a president with a majority in the Senate could nominate a more radical candidate, knowing he or she would be confirmed.

In 2017, the narrow Republican majority in the Senate used the nuclear option to confirm President Trump's choice of Supreme Court justice, the conservative judge Neil Gorsuch. Before the nuclear option was triggered, Oregon Senator Jeff Merkley spoke for more than 15 hours overnight against Gorsuch's appointment. However, Merkley's speech was not technically a filibuster, as it did not delay Senate legislative action. After three days of debate, Gorsuch was approved by 54 votes to 45.

Neil Gorsuch (right, back row) poses with his fellow Supreme Court justices after having his nomination confirmed. President Trump nominated him for his conservative views on many issues.

Chapter 5

CONTROVERSIES
AND DEBATES

Today, the filibuster is one of the most controversial elements of Senate proceedings. That is partly because of the way its use has changed since it was first introduced. Originally, it was intended to guarantee free speech by allowing every senator a chance to have a full say on an issue. Now, it is more often used as a political tool. Before cloture was introduced in 1917, senators used the filibuster to put across their point of view. Today, the filibuster is more often used to stop bills from being debated at all. That is a big change.

A Grinding Halt

Until the middle of the 1800s, the filibuster was barely used. There was so little legislation that the Senate had time to discuss bills for as long as necessary.

Senators discuss their tactics during a debate on an issue in the Senate chamber.

Political opinions in the Senate were not as **polarized** as they later became. By the 1880s, however, there was usually at least one obstruction during every two-year Congress. This relatively sparing use of the filibuster continued until 1975.

Government Shutdown

In 1975, new rules changed the nature of filibustering and allowed senators to carry on other business while a filibuster was under way. However, the

President Trump, who came to office in January 2017, was often frustrated by the delaying tactics of the Democratic minority.

introduction of this virtual filibuster did not remove the filibuster's power to disrupt government. In January 2018, the US government shut down after the Senate failed to reach the 60 votes needed to break a filibuster over a government funding bill. The Democratic minority filibustered to try to force Republicans to agree to protect immigrants who had been illegally brought to the United States as children.

When the bill did not pass, parts of the federal government stopped work. President Trump intervened by tweeting that Senate Republicans should adopt the nuclear option of allowing a majority of 51 votes. In fact, the three-day shutdown ended when Senate Republicans and Democrats agreed to try to reach an agreement over Dreamers impacted by the ending of the DACA program, which had given them the right to stay in the United States.

The government shutdown confirmed what many political observers suspected—the increasing use of filibusters reflected growing political divisions. Filibusters were now being used to prevent the Senate from doing its business.

One of the most visible signs of a government shutdown is the closure of attractions managed by the National Parks Service, such as Yosemite in California.

Making a Point

The filibuster can be very frustrating for government—yet most politicians are reluctant to get rid of it completely. For one thing, people's opinion of the filibuster varies according to whether they are in the majority or minority party. The majority, who know they will win a vote, see filibustering as a nuisance that wastes

Senator Chris Murphy filibustered in 2016 to try to force the Senate to debate increased gun control—but no change in legislation resulted.

time and stops the Senate from working efficiently. Minority members, however, see it as a valuable tool that allows them to have their say and potentially influence new legislation. Now that Senate proceedings are broadcast live on national TV, a filibuster is also a chance for a senator to make an impact by gaining public exposure. This keeps issues in the public eye while reminding citizens that politicians are doing their jobs in Congress.

WHAT DO YOU THINK?

Senators such as Rand Paul made their names by staging filibusters that raised their profiles in their own parties. What other ways can senators raise their profiles and advance their careers?

THE POWER OF THE PEOPLE

In the Texas State Senate in 2013, state senator Wendy Davis wore sneakers and a back brace during a filibuster. She stood and spoke for 13 hours nonstop in an attempt to delay the introduction of a ban on abortions after 20 weeks of pregnancy. Davis argued that it was a woman's right to decide when to end her pregnancy. She used the filibuster to get as wide an audience as possible for her message. Video of the event went viral across the United States and around the world—even though the bill she fought against ended up passing into law.

The Texas State Senate in Austin, Texas, has 31 senators, who each represent a district across the state. Each district has the same population: about 806,000 people.

I'm on TV!

The exposure a senator can get by filibustering is a source of criticism. Critics allege that some senators are less interested in politics than in having a moment in the **limelight**. While most senators do use the Senate floor to highlight

In Mr. Smith Goes to Washington, *James Stewart (right) plays a naive senator who filibusters for 24 hours.*

certain issues, critics of filibustering claim that others will talk about anything in order to gain personal attention. Such an attitude also reflects a romantic notion in which the filibuster is the means for an idealistic individual to take a stand against unscrupulous government. Such scenes sometimes appear in movies, most notably in *Mr. Smith Goes to Washington* (1939), in which James Stewart plays a new senator who speaks against a corrupt budget bill until he passes out.

WHAT DO YOU THINK?.

The filibuster scene in *Mr. Smith Goes to Washington* is very famous—but it is fictional. What are the possible dangers of learning about politics from movies and novels?

Chapter 6

FILIBUSTERS
AND YOU

What happens in Washington, D.C., and in the Senate might seem a long way from your daily life. However, the system of government means that what happens inside the US Senate matters to every American. The Senate is the senior chamber in which laws are debated and then passed. Some laws never make it through the Senate, and almost no laws pass without some kind of amendment. It is often senators who make those changes. The laws they make govern how Americans live.

This memorial was created after the shooting of 20 elementary schoolchildren and 6 teachers in Connecticut in 2012.

In 2010, Republicans filibustered to stop Democratic legislation to reduce pollution by cutting the use of fossil fuels.

Serious Issues

Filibusters have been used to block or try to change laws that affect many areas of everyday life, such as gun control. Following the mass shooting in Orlando, Florida, in June 2016, Senator Chris Murphy filibustered to force the Senate leadership to schedule votes on gun-control measures.

In February 2018, following the shooting of 17 people at a high school in Parkland, Florida, there were widespread calls for Congress to pass gun-control laws. The Senate has consistently failed to pass legislation, partly due to **lobbying** by the National Rifle Association (NRA). On March 23, 2018, President Trump signed the Fix NICS Act. The law forces federal and state agencies to share information about criminals and other people who should not be able to buy guns. For critics of gun ownership, the law does not go far enough—for which they blame the Senate.

In 2018, some minimum-wage workers still earned a pay rate of $7.25, which was set in 2009.

The Minimum Wage

For millions of Americans who work in low-paid jobs, a guaranteed hourly wage is vital. In 2014, Republicans in the Senate launched a filibuster to stop a Democrat proposal that would have introduced a federal minimum wage of $10.10 per hour. The bill did not pass, but many states have chosen to set their own minimum wages.

WHAT DO YOU THINK?

Many Americans believe the government should not interfere in issues such as how much an employer pays his or her workers. What other ways might there be to achieve, for instance, fairer pay for women?

THE POWER OF THE PEOPLE

Everybody wants to earn a fair wage for their work. But in 2014, Republicans filibustered a proposal to raise the minimum federal wage. Politicians in many states took their own actions. In January 2018, 29 states had a state minimum wage that was higher than the federal minimum of $7.25, which had been in place since 2009. Cities such as New York, Los Angeles, and Washington, D.C., also set their own minimum wages, because they recognized that the cost of living is higher in cities.

Opponents of raising minimum wage say that it raises costs for employers, which means that ultimately employers create fewer jobs. Supporters argue that it prevents exploitation of workers.

Taxes and Pay

In the past, Republicans also blocked other legislation that directly affected Americans. In 2012, they filibustered to stop the "Buffet Rule." This measure, named for the wealthy investor Warren Buffet who supported it, would have levied a minimum tax on the wealthiest Americans.

In 2014, Republicans filibustered another attempt by Democrats to change legislation about pay. They blocked the Paycheck Fairness Act four times. The act was aimed at making it harder for employers to pay women less than men for doing the same job.

Protestors march in support of the "Buffet Rule," which would have placed much higher taxes on wealthy Americans.

WHAT DO YOU THINK?

The Buffet Rule was named for the investor Warren Buffet. Do you think successful businesspeople such as Buffet can play a useful role in US politics? What sort of contribution might they be able to make?

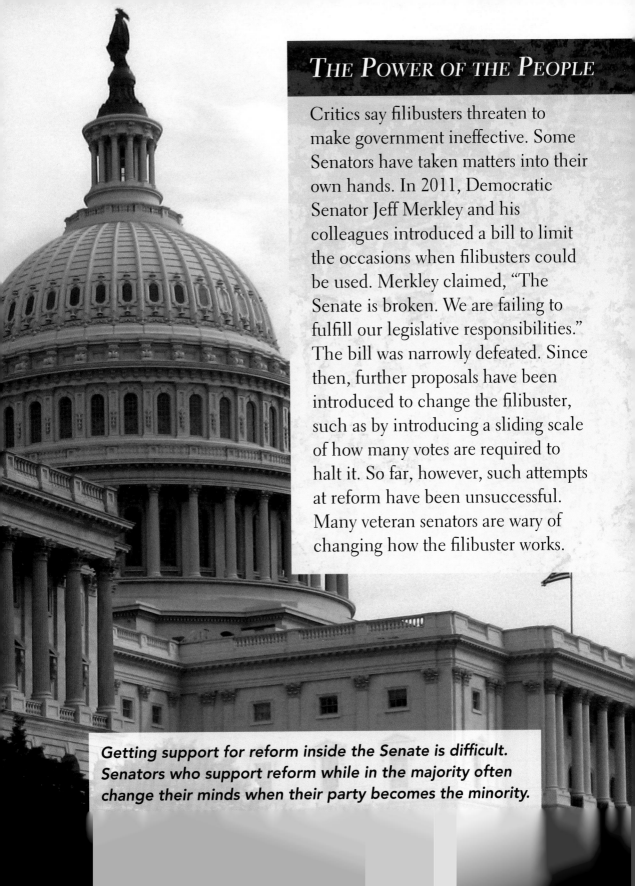

THE POWER OF THE PEOPLE

Critics say filibusters threaten to make government ineffective. Some Senators have taken matters into their own hands. In 2011, Democratic Senator Jeff Merkley and his colleagues introduced a bill to limit the occasions when filibusters could be used. Merkley claimed, "The Senate is broken. We are failing to fulfill our legislative responsibilities." The bill was narrowly defeated. Since then, further proposals have been introduced to change the filibuster, such as by introducing a sliding scale of how many votes are required to halt it. So far, however, such attempts at reform have been unsuccessful. Many veteran senators are wary of changing how the filibuster works.

Getting support for reform inside the Senate is difficult. Senators who support reform while in the majority often change their minds when their party becomes the minority.

Chapter 7

GETTING
INVOLVED

Filibustering is an important part of our political system. It has been around for more than 200 years. Only senators can technically carry out a filibuster, which might make it seem difficult for ordinary citizens to become involved. However, filibusters are closely entwined with the business of government. As such, all voters should have a close interest in them.

How would you feel if one of your elected representatives began to read out recipes rather than debate important political issues? Should such tactics have a place in US politics?

Voters can influence filibusters. They can put pressure on their senators to try to delay or change legislation. This is also possible in state government, where many state constitutions also allow senators to filibuster to prevent issues coming to a vote. Every citizen is free to write to or meet with their elected representatives to suggest that they use a filibuster to prevent particular measures. There is, however, no obligation for that representative to agree to such action.

Like other senators, Ted Cruz of Texas supported filibusters when his party was the minority in the Senate. He opposed them when he became part of the majority.

Your Own Filibuster

On a local level, it might even be possible to become involved in a filibuster yourself. Some local organizations such as school boards or town councils have rules based loosely on those of Congress. If you object to particular measures, find out whether a procedure exists that would allow you, a group of friends, or a designated spokesperson to delay a vote.

For or Against?

Many people believe the filibuster is misused to slow down legislation. However, others say the filibuster is more necessary than ever. Today, decisions about which bills are voted on are made among a leadership group headed by the Majority leader. Most senators are excluded from these decisions. They only have one means of getting their voice heard: the filibuster. According to this view, suggestions that the filibuster should be removed would destroy a vital part of democracy in the United States. If you feel strongly about the issue, you could write to your senator to tell him or her whether or not you believe the system needs to be changed.

The US Supreme Court makes the ultimate decisions about whether laws are constitutional or not.

WHAT DO YOU THINK?

If enough electors believe a politician is doing a bad job, they can demand a recall election, in which he or she might be defeated. What sort of issues might make you support a recall election?

THE POWER OF THE PEOPLE

Is there an issue that you feel strongly about? Does it concern your state, the nation, or the whole world? Do you think your elected representatives are doing enough to raise the issue in Congress or in your local state Senate? One way to make sure they do is to write them. Explain why you think they should be talking about a particular issue. Get your friends to email or write their own letters. You never know: maybe your representative will become the next to filibuster on the Senate floor.

Senators listen to a presidential address to Congress. It is their responsibility to react to voters' concerns—even if it means delaying or obstructing legislation.

Glossary

assassinated: murdered for political reasons

bacteria: tiny organisms that are responsible for causing disease

bipartisan: involving the agreement of two political parties that usually oppose each other

debate: a formal discussion in government that ends with a vote on a particular issue

Dreamers: children brought to the United States by parents who were illegal immigrants

drones: unpiloted aerial vehicles that are controlled by an operator on the ground, or by a computer program

intelligence services: government agencies responsible for gathering information on other countries and protecting their own country against spying

legislation: a law or group of laws

limelight: public attention

lobbying: attempting to influence political or other leaders to create or change particular legislation

lucrative: paying well

lynching: the killing of someone for an alleged crime without a trial

polarized: divided into two completely opposite groups

recession: a period of economic decline, when trade and industrial activity fall

For More Information

Books

McAuliffe, Bill. *The U.S. Senate.* We the People. Mankato, MN: Creative Education, 2016.

Small, Cathleen. *How Does Congress Work?* American Democracy in Action. New York: Lucent Books, 2018.

Spalding, Maddie. *How the Legislative Branch Works.* How America Works. Mankato, MN: Child's World Inc., 2016.

Websites

Gallery of Filibusters
http://vanwinkles.com/10-longest-filibusters-in-senate-history
A list of the 10 longest filibusters in the US Senate, with video links.

How Stuff Works
https://people.howstuffworks.com/filibuster.htm
An article about how the filibuster works and how politicians have used it over history.

Index